The Heart of Missionary Theology

G. Christian Weiss

MOODY PRESS
CHICAGO

Moody Press Edition, 1977

Library of Congress Cataloging in Publication Data

Weiss, George Christian, 1910-
    The heart of missionary theology.

    1. Missions—Theory.   2. Missions—Biblical
teaching.   I. Title.
BV2063.W44   1977   266'.001   77-1967
ISBN 0-8024-3483-5

Printed in the United States of America

Contents

Introduction

This book is not intended to be a comprehensive treatise on Christian theology or even on missionary theology. An exhaustive work would obviously require far more space than this document affords. Dr. George W. Peters has done a masterful job of dealing with the subject in his book *A Biblical Theology of Missions* (Moody Press).

Neither is this a philosophical work, such as an exhaustive or profound treatment of the subject would require. And it is not a complete biblical study on the subject of missionary theology. Rather, this is an analytical study based mainly on one significant passage of scripture—one that is often overlooked in the study of biblical theology. However, it is our purpose to embrace the general scope of biblical teaching on the subject and to be in complete accord with it.

It is an indictment against evangelicals that their theologians have been tardy in entering this extremely important literary field. In the past they have neglected this area of study while liberals have gone to press with their views and interpretations of the Scriptures and of our Christian mission. However, it is gratifying to know that some recent evangelical works are available, though not as many as those produced by writers whose evangelical position is questionable.

Our purpose here is to provide the average Christian lay person with a handbook based on the Scriptures and designed to clarify a vital area of truth and to stimulate more in-depth Bible study. In short, this is designed to be a handbook, not an exhaustive textbook, on the theology of the Christian mission. As the title suggests, this document deals with the heart of missionary theology rather than the total body of it. I wish to plant kernels of seed in the hope that they will grow into full ears in the minds and lives of Christians who read this book.

One more comment should be made here—about the word "mission." Evangelicals habitually refer to the enterprise of world evangelization as "missions." They often become suspicious of the use of "mission," "our mission," "the Christian mission" and similar terms. This is not because the terms have any basic faults but because they have been commonly used by liberals and by certain pseudo-evangelicals. But should we allow good terms and titles to be removed from correct usage simply because they are used by people who do not agree with fundamental biblical Christianity? After all, these same people use other essential titles and terms common among all Christians, such as prayer, faith, redemption, the gospel and salvation.

The casual way in which the word "missions" is used among evangelical Christians often conveys a concept far below and out of keeping with the great task of publishing the good news of salvation in Jesus Christ to the world and taking out of the nations a people for His name. The term tends to convey the idea of segregated, specific efforts of missionaries here and there in overseas countries, such as a mission station, a clinic, a school, a leprosarium, a radio station, a printing operation or whatever. But these are only individual efforts made toward the one great mission of Christ's Church, which is the evangelization of the world. Even the old slogan "The mission of the Church is missions" is not completely accurate. The mission of the Church is the evangelization of the world.

Why should we not use the perfectly correct term "the Christian mission"? After all, Jesus assigned but one mission to His Church, and He clearly defined that mission when He committed it to the apostles: "Go ye therefore, and teach [make disciples of] all nations, baptizing them in the name of the Father, and of the Son, and of the Holy Ghost: teaching them to observe all things whatsoever I have commanded you: and, lo, I am with you alway, even unto the end of the world" (Matt, 28:19,20). "Go ye unto all the world, and preach [proclaim] the gospel to every creature" (Mark 16:15). "It is written, . . . that repentance and remission of sins should be preached in his name among all nations. . . . And ye are witnesses of these things" (Luke 24:46-48). "Ye shall be witnesses unto me both in Jerusalem, and in all Judaea, and in Samaria, and unto the uttermost part of the earth" (Acts 1:8).

Therefore, the mission of the Church is clear, and its performance was to begin on the day of Pentecost when the Holy Spirit came. Believers are to preach the Gospel to all the nations of the world and to make Christian disciples from among the nations. This is correctly called the evangelization of the world. Even though definitions of world evangelization may be variously interpreted and defined by different persons, whatever Jesus meant by assigning to the apostles that task constitutes the mission of the Church.

The historic Westminister Confession and the famed catechisms based on it properly stipulate that the Bible alone is the basis of faith and practice for the Christian in all things. In this volume we are particularly concerned that Christian people clearly understand what the Bible teaches about world evangelization. Unless they have such an understanding, they will not likely have a solid conviction or a deep interest regarding world missionary endeavors.

A somewhat common attitude among Christians is that although missionaries are sincere, zealous, even heroic people, they are not necessarily or generally capable Bible scholars. I well remember being in a conference where a sharp distinction was drawn, by the directors, between missionaries and Bible teachers. These leaders assumed that a missionary was not a Bible teacher. The inference might also have been that the Bible teacher was not a missionary. At least such proved to be the case in that particular conference.

But that which actually makes Christian men and women become genuine missionaries is their arrival at certain unshakable convictions from the Bible regarding God's world plan and their Christian responsibility toward the world according to that plan. These convictions drive them to the mission field in the first place and keep them on the field year after year in faithful, selfless service. The mere spirit of adventure or philanthropy is not sufficient to do this. But an understanding of the teachings of Scripture and the sound conviction of its demands on believers will not allow the missionary to do otherwise.

ONE

Universal Prayer

The Bible portions that have come to mean the most to me through the years are the following great passages: Genesis 12, where the call of God to Abraham and His purpose for the nation of Israel are recorded; Luke 24:45-49, which contains a real key to understanding the Scriptures; John 6, where Christ's mission to a hungry and bewildered world is vividly portrayed and plainly explained by Him; Romans 1—8, which contains the touchstone of the Gospel and of Christian living; and 1 Timothy 2:1-8. We will be dealing basically with this passage from 1 Timothy in this treatise. In these unique verses we encounter the cardinal doctrines of the entire Bible—the essence of basic Christian teaching. It is not an unwarranted presumption or a misnomer to title this portion of Scripture "The Heart of Missionary Theology."

Seven important Christian doctrines are mentioned or alluded to in this passage. First, prayer in behalf of all people is entreated. Universal prayer is asked of the Christian; it is, in fact, the apostle's first and major injunction in the passage. Second, the unequivocal truth of the unity of God is asserted. "There is one God" (v.5)—one God only. The inference is that all must come to know Him in truth in order to be saved. Third, the universal love and concern of God is asserted. The desire of God is that all people come to the knowledge and experience of salvation in Christ.

Fourth, it is affirmed that there is only one mediator between God and His human creatures. Therefore, all must come to God through Jesus Christ. Fifth, it is asserted in this passage that this unique mediator provided a ransom for all—that His atonement was universal. Sixth, it is stated that the redemption of Jesus Christ is to be shared with all mankind—the "all" for whom He gave Himself as ransom. Seventh, it is clearly shown that human instrumentality is God's ordained method for doing this. He uses people, of whom the apostle Paul was one.

In this opening study we will consider the first of these great truths: Prayer for all people is urged on Christians. The apostle enjoined universal prayer by saying, "I exhort therefore, that, first of all, supplications, prayers, intercessions, and giving of thanks, be made for all men" (v.1). The expression "first of all" probably refers to the order in which the apostle made important exhortations to his son in the faith. But it also quite obviously signifies that prayer is of first importance. The famed Greek scholar Dr. A. T. Robertson asserts this in his *Word Pictures in the New Testament* (Broadman). I regard Paul's expression "first of all" as the equivalent of our saying something like "in the first place," implying major importance.

Prayer is an integral element in the Christian faith and a basic tenet in Christian theology. Prayer is, in fact, an element of virtually all religions, but in a unique sense it is essential to Christianity. Here it is the personal petitions of individual believers to an almighty God who is transcendent and benevolent. Genuine prayer embraces petition, intercession, and thanksgiving, all of which are included in the apostolic exhortation in this passage. All of these have a place in the experience of every true Christian.

The strong point made about prayer in this portion of Scripture is that the believer is to pray for "all men." This is where true missionary vision and work begin. And it is the part of that mission in which any and every individual Christian may participate, no matter how limited he may be in other areas.

In 2 Timothy, Paul wrote: "The things that thou hast heard of me . . . the same commit thou to faithful men, who shall be able to teach others also" (2:2). This certainly includes the important exhortation to pray for all people. Prayer is to be universal in two respects: It is to be universal among Christians—all Christians are to pray—and they are to pray universally for all people.

The casual reader might regard this exhortation as a mere pious platitude. But to the serious Bible reader such an attitude is repugnant and instantly rejected. Rather than being a pious platitude, it spells out the practical participation of the Christian in the mission of the Church—the bringing of everyone to the knowledge of the truth of God and our Saviour. As previously stated, this is where the missionary vision of any Christian begins—at the throne of grace. But anything that begins in prayer never ends with prayer. Intercession leads to action. Genuine prayer for all people, which is here exhorted by the apostle Paul, always leads to actual endeavor in behalf of the spiritual welfare of all people. Intercession is a basic element of Christian theology and also a practical element in active Christianity.

Some may ask, How can we pray for *all* people? How can we pray for people whom we do not know, whom we have never seen, and whom we have not even heard about? Even though this may be a problem to the rationalistic theologian, it is no problem to the individual Christian. Many have done this. And this is where the Christian mission begins. We can pray that all those who have no knowledge of the true God and of salvation in Jesus Christ may, according to God's will, come to know the truth and be saved.

After giving the exhortation that prayer be made for all people and marking its importance as "first of all," the apostle went on to say, "This is good and acceptable in the sight of God our Saviour; who will have all men to be saved, and to come unto the knowledge of the truth" (vv. 3-4). This is precisely the great burden behind this passage of Scripture. And this must be a cardinal element in Christian theology and experience.

The apostle's use of the word "intercessions" is significant. Intercession is without doubt the very highest form of prayer. We are exhorted to intercede for people's salvation, for their spiritual deliverance. This we are to do for everyone.

How many Christians actually pray this way? How many pray for the whole world for "all men"? Yet this is a clear, unmistakable injunction of God's Word. It is something Christians are exhorted to do and something they can do. Many may sincerely feel that they have an excuse for not going into missionary service. Some may have legitimate excuses for not being able to give much. But who among God's people can excuse themselves from prayer for the world, for all mankind, for the heathen? The humblest and most restricted Christian in the world can still pray, and he can pray for others; he can pray for the world.

An exhortation of this nature may, on the surface, seem to be out of keeping with the title of this book— *The Heart of Missionary Theology*. But theology is not primarily concerned with tenets that merely receive mental assent but with truths that reach into the heart and affect the life. Any treatise or portion of theology that fails to do this is of little practical value. That is why Paul began this very significant statement in 1 Timothy with an exhortation to universal prayer.

Many humble Christian people have a plan to regularly pray for the needs of mission fields around the world. For this very purpose mission boards put out prayer calendars. These guide Christians into regular intercession for the work of the mission including missionary personnel and the people in their fields to whom they are bringing the gospel. This is putting Christian theology into practice, and theology in action is the only worthwhile kind.

A more thorough examination of this first exhortation is in order. Note that the language the apostle used is extremely forceful. "I exhort therefore, that, first of all, supplications, prayers, intercessions, . . . be made for all men" (v.1). The word "exhort" is a very strong one. It means "to urge, to plead, to press upon." Very literally it means "to urge out." The apostle was actually saying, "I urge out of my soul, out of my inner being, that you pray for all men!" It expresses deep concern and desire and also implies profound importance.

And we must not overlook the significance of "first of all." He exhorts believers to pray before all else—not last but first. We are naturally prone to think of everything else first and to give attention to prayer as something supplemental. We devise our programs, we undertake a lot of actions, and then at the end we ask God's blessing on what we have planned or done. This is not the right order. The apostle Paul urged "first of all,—prayer" (v. 1). As stated above, this refers

13

to both time **and priority. Prayer is to be** first of all, **above** all, before all, in all.

One more fact must be observed at this point. Paul proceeded from exhorting to prayer for all to soliciting particular and special prayer "for kings, and for all that are in authority; that we may lead a quiet and peaceable life in all godliness and honesty" (v. 2). This specific instruction indicates that prayer for political rulers is highly significant.

When one studies the life of this apostle, however, one does not get the impression that this great man was primarily interested in a comfortable and quiet life! No one who honestly reads the New Testament could get such an impression. In many of the places where Paul preached, riots and tumults occurred. He and his companions were called "these that have turned the world upside down" (Acts 17:6). The account of his life in the book of the Acts, as well as his own testimonies in 2 Corinthians 4 and 11, indicates that he experienced anything but a quiet and peaceable life. He was ready and willing to go through anything and everything for Jesus' sake. And he did exactly that.

Why, therefore, did he make a request for "a quiet and peaceable life"? (1 Tim 2:2). The answer is clearly implied in the passage. He exhorted prayer for kings and for all in authority in order that believers might have political quiet and peace so that they could, in all honesty and liberty, go on proclaiming the message of Jesus Christ to the whole world—to all nations, people, and places.

Paul was living under the reign of the notorious Emperor Nero. The Roman Empire was a great world empire at the time. It controlled the lives and circumstances of masses of people in the then-known world. Paul was concerned that people throughout this great empire might receive the knowledge of the true God and the saving knowledge of Jesus Christ. Therefore, he exhorted Christians to pray that the rulers and those in authority might not hinder the work of world evangelization. He desired liberty, freedom, and peace so that he and others could go on proclaiming the gospel of Christ without hindrance. This must be the significance of the statement relating to living "in all godliness and honesty" (v.2). He desired to live and carry on his work as a Christian witness with uprightness and a good conscience before the laws and government.

W. W. Wessel has this comment: "Verses 2 through 4 seem to suggest that the Christian desire for a quiet and peaceable life is in order to practice godliness and that full opportunity may be given to propogate the gospel."

Commentary Critical and Explanatory on the Whole Bible, by Robert Jamieson, A. R. Fausset, and David Brown, states that the word "quiet" implies "not troubled from without." It comments that the quiet of Christians at that time was dependent in a particular way on subordinate rulers more than on the supreme ruler in Rome.

These are days when this exhortation comes home to God's people in a very positive way. Right now is a volatile time for world evangelization and, therefore, a highly critical time in which to pray for those who are in authority in the governments of the world. Many in high places of government are not people of God and do not know or honor Jesus Christ. Some of the world's chief rulers today deny the very existence of God; they are militant atheists. Some of these hold literally hundreds of millions of people in their power and are aggresively trying to keep any Christian witness or portion of God's Word from reaching them.

Christians in today's world must heed this exhortation to pray for these leaders so that the servants of Jesus Christ in these areas may be able to publicly preach the Gospel. It is a conscience-probing thing to have to preach the Gospel in defiance of human law or use devious methods of circumventing the laws of the land to carry on the work of evangelization. Messengers of Christ's Gospel long to work without restriction as they proclaim His message to mankind.

This, then, is the first great truth in this all-embracing passage of Scripture—prayer for all people in the world. Christians are to pray that people will be delivered from the power of darkness and sin, that they will come to the true knowledge of Jesus Christ through God's Word, and that the rulers of the world will be guided by the over-ruling hand of God so they will not do things that could throw the world into jeopardy. Prayer for peace and freedom to go on with the task of proclaiming the Gospel of Jesus Christ throughout the earth is a fundamental element of true Christian doctrine and experience.

TWO

The Unity of God

The unity of God is one of the central truths of 1 Timothy 2:1-8: "There is one God" (v.5).

The meaning is clear: There is only one God.

The unity of God is theologically termed *monotheism*. *Mono* signifies the singular, one. And *theos* is the Greek word for God. Monotheism, therefore, means "the belief in one God." Opposite to this is the pagan belief in polytheism, or belief in many gods.

Monotheism is basic to every tenet of Christian theology. No other concept is admissible to Christian belief. The entire empahsis of the Bible is monotheistic. (The triune nature of this one God, strongly inferred in the Old Testament and clearly taught in the New Testament, is outside the scope of our present discussion.)

The Old Testament emphatically teaches unmixed monotheism. God is one, and there is no other. The famous *Shema* (the Jewish confession of faith) consists of the words God spoke to the people of ancient Israel through His servant Moses: "Hear, O Israel: The Lord our God is one Lord" (Deut 6:4). The passage continues: "Thou shalt fear the LORD thy God, and serve him, and shalt swear by his name. Ye shall not go after other gods, of the gods of the people which are round about you" (vv. 13, 14).

This passage emphasizes that there is one God and one God only. Therefore, love Him; there is no other

God to love. Serve **Him; there is no other** Sovereign Master. Worship Him; there is no other God to worship. Trust Him; there is no other God to help you.

The One revealed as Jehovah in the Old Testament is not a tribal deity of the Hebrew people. He is set forth as the creator and sovereign of all mankind. He is revealed as the only true and living God of the whole earth. This is the consistent teaching and emphasis of the Old Testament scriptures. The main course of sin warned against throughout the Old Testament is polytheism and idolatry. The people of Israel were solemnly warned against participating in the worship of other so-called gods, and they were severely judged when they disobeyed this command. The Babylonian Exile is an outstanding example from the Old Testament of God's judgment on them for such participation.

In the New Testament the emphasis is the same: There is one God. Paul wrote: "We know that an idol is nothing in the world, and that there is none other God but one. For though there be that are called gods, whether in heaven or in earth, (as there be gods many, and lords many,) but to us there is but one God, the Father, of whom are all things, and we in him; and one Lord Jesus Christ, by whom are all things, and we by him" (1 Cor 8:4-6). The New Testament clearly declares that there is "one Lord, one faith, one baptism, one God and Father of all, who is above all, and through all, and in you all" (Eph 4:5-6). And in 1 Timothy we are confronted by Paul's firm statement to Timothy: "There is one God" (2:5).

Throughout the entire Bible heathenism is totally repudiated and rejected. The worship of pagan gods is termed vain and useless. It is, in fact, evil and symbolized as spiritual adultery. It is repeatedly referred to as an abomination and utterly rejected by the true, living God. Heathen religions are referred to as religions of darkness, and the people who follow other gods are said to be walking in spiritual darkness (see Eph 4:18; 2:12).

The concept of monotheism logically and automatically demands the missionary concept. Any religions that hold to the concept of a tribal or local deity obviously do not embrace the concept of missions as something inevitable. If the god worshiped is exclusive to one's own people, and other tribes and nations have gods of their own, all missionary incentive is automatically eliminated. But all through the Scriptures we see the opposite emphasis—that Jehovah is the God of all mankind. Therefore, since He is the one and only true God, and since all other gods are vain, the truth concerning Him ought to be proclaimed to all mankind. This is taught in the Bible as a basic fact, a truth relevant to all human life. All people are of necessity connected with God because there is no other God. He must be the Creator of all people, and all are connected with Him by virtue of their very creation.

He must also be the sole Sustainer of human life. The Bible affirms clearly, "In him we live, and move, and have our being (Acts 17:28). And we are told that He is the One "with whom we have to do" (Heb 4:13). This verse says, "all things are naked and opened unto the eyes of him with whom we have to do." People have a certain relationship to the God of the Bible; they have to give account to the one and only God set forth in the Old and New Testaments.

People are related to God here in this life. God has a will, and He has revealed His will in His Book. Human lives are necessarily related to that re-

19

vealed will. They are either lived in harmony with the divine will or they are lived contrary to it.

Even for our physical sustenance we have a dependent relationship to God. God makes the heart beat. He gives us air to breathe and power to breathe it. He gives us physical strength and well-being. He causes the earth to bring forth the produce by which human life is sustained. All things, even in the purely physical realm of life, come from His hands. There is no other ultimate source for these things.

And in the life to come—in eternity, forever— people will still have an inescapable relationship to God. After death comes judgment. This fact is not only asserted in the Scriptures but is universally lodged in the mind. People were made in God's image as free moral agents responsible for their lives and deeds. They must meet God, and He will judge them for the way they have lived on earth. Because of this, all people need to know Him. There is no other God. He is their God, their Creator, their life's Sovereign, and their Judge.

So the concept of monotheism—belief in one God—demands a missionary concept and missionary involvement. The Bible shows that, although God is man's Creator, the Father-son relationship between God and man has been disrupted. Sin has broken this relationship; it has separated man from God. The Bible, therefore, describes man as an alien from God and a stranger to His covenants, having no hope in the world and having corrupted his own way. We are told in Romans 1 that when people originally knew God, they would not worship Him or serve Him, and they were not grateful to Him. Instead, they became vain in their own imaginations, and their foolish minds were darkened (v. 21). They forsook God, and then they corrupted themselves. This is the story told in human history, repeated over and over again.

But the Bible also shows that, though all this is true and though man's character has sadly changed and deteriorated, God's character has not changed. His love continues uninterrupted. He loves all the children of men, despite their sin. His self-communicating mercy reaches to all mankind, and His call is still, "Look unto me, and be ye saved, all the ends of the earth: for I am God, and there is none else" (Isa 45:22). In this same wonderful invitation given through the prophet Isaiah, He declared, "There is no God else beside me; a just God and a Saviour; there is none beside me" (v. 21).

The Bible tells the wonderful story about the creator of the world, the divine, eternal *Logos* (Word), condescending to come to earth in the form of man to become man's Redeemer and Deliverer. Because of this redemptive work of Jesus Christ, God can again become man's true Father; this relationship takes place when an individual places personal trust in the Saviour and puts his faith in that Saviour as his own Sin-bearer and Redeemer.

This was the message that burned in the heart of the apostle Paul. When he specified, "There is one God" (1 Tim 2:5), he was not merely declaring a cold doctrine or an arbitrary religious dogma. Instead, he was asserting a burning truth: There is only one God; there is no other. Unless the people of the world come to know Him, they simply do not know God. Unless they come to this God for salvation, they can have no salvation. The gods of the pagans are hopeless and helpless. The gods of people's manufacturing are all nothing. They cannot answer a cry or meet a need.

There is only one God. Therefore, people must come to Him.

The concept of monotheism demands the concept of the Christian mission. Since there is only one true God and Saviour, and since there is no salvation or redemption outside of Him, people must be told the Gospel of God's love. They must know of His giving His only-begotten Son to redeem us so that whoever believes in Him should not perish but have everlasting life (see John 3:16).

THREE

The Universal Love and Concern of God

The premise we have laid for this book is that 1 Timothy 2:1-8 embraces the very heart of Christian missionary theology. As previously stated, this passage has the essence of most of the major Christian teachings: (1) universal prayer is enjoined in behalf of all people; (2) the essential unity of God is asserted; (3) the love and concern of God for mankind is declared; (4) the singularity of Christ's mediatorial work and ministry are specified; (5) the universality of His atonement is declared; (6) the universal proclamation of the Gospel is included; (7) human instrumentality is clearly alluded to.

In this chapter we will consider the third of these great Christian truths—the universal love and concern of God for mankind. First Timothy 2:3-4 reads: "This [prayer for all people] is good and acceptable in the sight of God our Saviour; who will have all men to be saved, and to come unto the knowledge of the truth."

This statement clearly and positively indicates God's universal love and concern for mankind. The only true God deeply loves all His human creatures and is concerned about their spiritual welfare and their relationship to Him. The passage asserts that He "will have all men to be saved" (v. 4). God's desire is that all be reconciled to Himself and be participants in His own eternal life and fellowship.

The *New American Standard Bible* translates this clause, "He desires all men to be saved" (v. 4). The meaning of the statement is clear: God's desire is that all be saved from the guilt, penalty, and power of their sins. While it is not stated that every individual will be saved, this passage does assert God's true desire for mankind—that all may come to the knowledge and joy of the salvation He has provided in Jesus Christ.

This most certainly proves His great love for all people. The one and only God, who is revealed in the Bible as the Creator and Sovereign of all, loves all and desires eternal salvation for all.

In fact, the love of God is a major theme of the Bible. Though this theme is not as prominent in the Old Testament as in the New Testament, it is nevertheless revealed in both. Early in the book of Genesis where man's creation and his original sinning against God are recorded, God appeared in the Garden of Eden, seeking the sinner who was separated from Him. He called to Adam, "Where art thou?" (3:9). God loved and sought man in spite of his willful disobedience and sin.

As a mouthpiece for God in his day, Jeremiah the prophet wrote these words: "I have loved thee with an everlasting love: therefore with lovingkindness have I drawn thee" (Jer 31:3). God's love, which is His own self-communication, forever reaches out toward wayward humanity, seeking to draw people to Himself as a hen would gather her chicks under her wing. Jesus used that very illustration when He wept over wayward Jerusalem (see Matt 23:37). Psalm 86 says that the Lord is "a God full of compassion, and gracious, longsuffering, and plenteous in mercy" (v. 15).

It is declared in the Old Testament that this boundless, wondrous love of God extends to all humanity. It reaches far beyond the boundaries of the people of Israel and embraces all the children of Adam's race. In the civil law given through Moses to Israel, God's love for other people was emphasized: "The stranger that dwelleth with you shall be unto you as one born among you, and thou shalt love him as thyself" (Lev 19:34). He wanted Israel to show grace and love to the strangers in their midst. They were not to forget or ignore the alien or the outsider that dwelt among them. Apparently, God wanted the ancient people of Israel to know that, even though they were His specially chosen ones and were recipients of particular promises and laws as His chosen instruments, they were not to forget their alien and pagan neighbors.

Through the prophet Isaiah, Jehovah said, "Look unto me, and be ye saved, all the ends of the earth: for I am God, and there is none else" (Isa 45:22). Here and repeatedly in the Old Testament we see God's universal love clearly manifested to the world.

In the New Testament, the love of God is a major theme. In the spirit of the entire New Testament, the apostle John wrote: "Beloved, let us love one another: for love is of God. . . . He that loveth not knoweth not God; for God is love. In this was manifested the love of God toward us, because that God sent his only begotten Son into the world, that we might live through him. Herein is love, not that we loved God, but that he loved us, and sent his Son to be the propitiation for our sins" (1 John 4:7-10). In a previous statement, the same apostle wrote: "And he [Christ] is the propitiation for our sins; and not for our's only, but also for the sins of the whole world" (2:2). In another place he exclaimed, "What manner of love the Father hath bestowed upon us, that we should be called the sons of God" (3:1).

This divine love is manifested toward all people.

The words of Jesus in the best-known verse of the entire Bible are these classic ones: "For God so loved the world, that he gave his only begotten Son, that whosoever believeth in him should not perish, but have everlasting life" (John 3:16). The eternal, universal love of God to man is a major emphasis throughout the New Testament. We are told that "the grace of God that bringeth salvation hath appeared to all men" (Titus 2:11).

It is beyond doubt that the divine love of God is a constant theme of the Bible and that it is particularly a major emphasis in the New Testament. Jesus' coming to die for the sins of the World, demonstrating the divine and universal love of God for the children of men, is the main New Testament message.

God's love has always been a major chord in Christian hymnology and worship. F. M. Lehman's song "The Love of God" speaks of the subject in highly descriptive terms.

Charles H. Gabriel wrote these lines:

> I stand amazed in the presence
> Of Jesus the Nazarene,
> And wonder how He could love me,
> A sinner condemned, unclean.
>
> How marvelous! How Wonderful
> And my song shall ever be:
> How marvelous! how wonderful
> Is my Savious's love for me!

The love of God is a distinctive to Christianity. It is a special revelation unique to the gospel of Jesus Christ. Most religions of the world have little, if any, concept of the love of God. The Muslims claim 99 names and titles for God in the Arabic language. On their prayer rosaries are 99 beads representing these 99 names, and they recite the 99 names repetitiously. But significantly and sadly, the name "Father" is not included among the 99. The concept of God as a gracious Father and the idea of a Father-son relationship with Him seems foreign to their understanding and theology.

Basically, this is true of most ethnic religions. The emphasis of these religions is principally on divine power, justice, and particularly wrath. Worship in pagan religions consists primarily of attempts to appease the anger of the deities. In sharp contrast to this the Bible emphasis, particularly that of the New Testament, is that God is love. It is His very nature to love. He is the essence of love. His love is seen as His self-communication to fallen mankind.

A comment on the second phrase of 1 Timothy 2:4 is required. The verse says that God "will have all men to be saved, and to come unto the knowledge of the truth." This implies that the love of God embraces His desire for all people to know the truth about Himself so that they can be saved. The meaning is not to first get saved and then come to the knowledge of the truth. Rather, it is a statement in apposition; the real meaning is that people are saved by coming to the knowledge of the truth. And this is God's desire for all. A respected commentator has defined the meaning of this as "To come to a precise and experimental knowledge of the truth."

God was grieved when sin broke the relationship between Himself and man, who had been created in His own divine image. And He longed to bring people back into a personal and experiential knowledge of Himself. The Bible very distinctly refers to the creator's grief over human sin and apostasy. It tells us, "God saw that the wickedness of man was great in the earth. . . .

And it grieved him at his heart" (Gen 6:5,6). This divine grief was most vividly expressed when Jesus lamented over Jerusalem and cried, "O Jerusalem, Jerusalem, . . . how often would I have gathered thy children together, even as a hen gathereth her chickens under her wings, and ye would not!" (Matt 23:37). Remember that only love can be grieved. Because God loves people, He is grieved at their sin. If He had hated man, He would not grieve. But because He loves us, our sin grieves His heart.

In order for people to be saved from their sins, they must come to a knowledge of God. They must have true knowledge of the only God and of Jesus Christ, the Son whom the Father sent into the world to be our Redeemer. The worship of idols and false gods will not suffice. The true and living God does not accept such worship. People must come to a personal knowledge and a personal relationship to the one and only true God, revealed in the Bible.

This demands world evangelization. It demands a worldwide mission. The mission of proclaiming the Gospel throughout the world is an essential element in the salvation of mankind. This message must go to all so that they may come to the knowledge of God in a personal, experiential way. The words of Jesus in His prayer to the Father before His arrest and crucifixion clearly show this. In that great intercessory prayer He said, "This is life eternal, that they might know thee the only true God, and Jesus Christ, whom thou hast sent" (John 17:3). In the same prayer He uttered the deep desire of His soul: "That the world may believe that thou hast sent me" (v. 21). From the depths of His soul He lamented, "O righteous Father, the world hath not known thee" (v. 25).

"Christian mission is cooperation with divine love." This statement is indisputably true. Hence this personal question: Are you in cooperation with God's love for the world? Is your church in cooperation with the love of God? Is your life in cooperation with divine love? Are your ambitions, desires, and goals in life in cooperation with His love?

FOUR

The Unique Mediatorship of Jesus Christ

A fourth cardinal truth of the gospel stated in 1 Timothy 2:1-8 is that Christ is the only mediator between God and man. "There is . . . one mediator between God and men, the man Christ Jesus" (v. 5). In this chapter we will consider the uniqueness of Christ's mediatorial position and ministry.

First, we need to define the word "mediator." It comes from the Latin word "media," meaning "the middle." Our great super highways illustrate this definition. As one travels down any of these super highways, he periodically sees signs which say, "Keep Off the Median." The median, of course, is the middle area between the two separate rights-of-way. It is the position or area between. A mediator is a go-between.

A mediator, therefore, is one who stands in the middle, or between two parties or entities. And he stands between them for the purpose of effecting a oneness, or harmony, between them.

A modern mediation board is an example. When a labor union strikes against the management of an industrial concern and the two parties cannot come to an agreement, the matter may be referred to an officially appointed board of arbitrators called the "mediation board." Such a board is sometimes appointed by the government. It stands between the two disagreeing parties and tries to effect a mutual agreement. An effective mediation board must break down any existing barriers between the two parties and bring them into harmony.

This is an illustration of a mediator. He is one who stands between two disagreeing parties for the purpose of reconciling them. The apostle Paul applied this definition to our Lord Jesus Christ, stating, "There is one God, and one mediator between God and men, the man Christ Jesus" (v. 5). Jesus Christ, by divine appointment and by virtue of His worth and ability, fills the office of Mediator between a holy God and sinful people.

A mediator is needed because of the breach caused by sin between God and man. As previously pointed out, this breach began when Adam first disobeyed God and acted contrary to His will. Immediately, a gap was created between the sinning creature and his divine Creator. The breach was actually a mutual one. Adam ran away to hide from God because he was afraid; then God put Adam out of the Garden of Eden because of his fallen and defiled nature. Adam ran from God, and God was compelled by His own holiness and justice to turn from Adam.

The great breach which thus began has continued down through human history. Centuries after Adam, the prophet Isaiah made this solemn declaration: "Behold, the LORD's hand is not shortened, that it cannot save; neither his ear heavy, that it cannot hear: but your iniquities have separated between you and your God, and your sins have hid his face from you, that he will not hear. For your hands are defiled with blood, and your fingers with iniquity; your lips have spoken lies, your tongue hath muttered perverseness. . . . Therefore is judgment far from us, neither doth justice overtake us: we wait for light, but behold obscurity; for brightness, but we walk in darkness. We grope for the wall like the blind, and we grope as if we had no eyes: we stumble at noon day as in the night; we are in desolate places as dead men. ... In transgressing and lying against the LORD, and departing away from our God, speaking oppression and revolt, conceiving and uttering from the heart words of falsehood.... The LORD saw it, and it displeased him" (Isa 59:1-3, 9, 10, 13, 15).

This passage and many more indicate the terrible gap that has occurred between God and man because of sin.

In Paul's epistle to the Romans we are told that the carnal, natural mind of man is "enmity against God: for it is not subject to the law of God, neither indeed can be" (8:7). The mind of sinful man is rebellious and disobedient against God. It is horridly depraved. We are also told that Christ came to reconcile us when we were enemies of God (see 5:10). Sinful humanity is at enmity with God, and every sinner is, in fact, a personal enemy of God. All who are following the course of sin and Satan and refusing to walk according to the revealed divine will are in rebellion against God. Sin is revolt against a holy, righteous God and against His perfect will.

The Bible emphatically declares that people are alienated from God because of their sin and the consequent blindness of their hearts and the darkening of their understanding. Paul, writing to the Colossians, said, "You ... were sometime [formerly] alienated and enemies in your mind by wicked works" (1:21). All such passages indicate the breach between God and man and show that this breach amounts to actual enmity.

The breach of sin involves all people. It separates

every person from God because all have sinned. The Scriptures include the heathen. To understand the full impact of many passages of Scripture, it must be remembered that, in Bible times (particularly New Testament times), the word *Gentile* indicated the pagan nations which were without the benefit of divine revelation and knowledge of God.

With this in mind, consider the truth of just two passages of Scripture, both in Paul's epistle to the Ephesians. Ephesians 2:11-12 says, "Wherefore remember, that ye being in time past Gentiles in the flesh, . . . at that time ye were without Christ, being aliens from the commonwealth of Israel, and strangers from the covenants of promise, having no hope, and without God in the world." The second passage is Ephesians 4:17-18: "Henceforth walk not as other Gentiles walk, in the vanity of their mind, having the understanding darkened, being alienated from the life of God through the ignorance that is in them, because of the blindness of their heart." For a detailed explanation and description of the gulf between God and all people, including the pagans, study Romans 1:18-32.

The wonder of God's grace and the Gospel is that, before man was ever created, Jesus Christ was ordained to become the great mediator—the go-between, the advocate, the reconciler, the peacemaker—between a holy, righteous God and sinful, depraved man. In order to fulfill this divine assignment, it was necessary for Him to become "the man Christ Jesus" (1 Tim 2:5). Under no circumstances must we bypass the importance of that term "the man."

To be an effective mediator between God and man, Jesus Christ had to take the form and characteristics of a man upon Himself. In order to negotiate from both the human side and the divine side of the breach, He had to be on an equal plane with both God and man. The incarnation of the Son of God in human flesh was essential to His mediatorial and redemptive work. Paul called this "the mystery of godliness: God was manifest in the flesh" (3:16). And indeed it is a mystery, a great mystery that is beyond full human comprehension.

The Bible sublimely states the mystery in these simple words: "Christ Jesus . . . being in the form of God, thought it not [a thing to be grasped]to be equal with God: but made himself of no reputation [emptied Himself], and took upon him the form of a servant, and was made in the likeness of men" (Phil 2:5-7). The same inspired author stated, "His Son Jesus Christ our Lord . . . was made of the seed of David according to the flesh" (Rom 1:3).

A biblical principle is stated in Hebrews: "Without shedding of blood is no remission" (9:22). Though that epistle refers to the long period of animal sacrifices required by the Mosaic law, it emphatically states, "It is not possible that the blood of bulls and of goats should take away sins" (10:4). Then Jesus Christ is introduced as the One for whom a body was prepared by the heavenly Father in order that He, by the sacrifice of Himself, might put away sin forever (see 9:1—10:18). It is not at all difficult to understand why a holy God could not accept the substitute of an innocent dumb animal for the sins of guilty, responsible people. But the eternal Son of God became a man to make peace between man and God through the shedding of His own blood.

Because He was Himself deity, Christ possessed the capability of paying the infinite price for human sin, a price that man could pay only by eternal condemnation and separation from God. And because He was man, Christ possessed the capability of taking upon Himself the sins of man. He was both able and willing to take the place of the guilty sinner and die for the sins of man, thus effecting a reconciliation between guilty mankind and the holy Creator.

The New Testament tells us that He "[blotted] out the handwriting of ordinances that was against us, which was contrary to us [the Law, which condemned us for our sins], and took it out of the way, nailing it to his cross" (Col 2:14). In the great passage that vividly depicts His incarnation and atonement, we are told that He "humbled himself, and became obedient unto death, even the death of the cross" (Phil 2:8). The apostle Peter wrote that He "suffered for sins, the just for the unjust, that he might bring us to God" (1 Pet 3:18).

How wonderful and marvelous it is that the eternal Son of God, the agent in the creation of the world and man, should stoop to identify Himself with His sinning creatures in order to become their Redeemer! He stooped down and made Himself one with us in our humanity so that we might be lifted up and be identified with Him in His divinity (see Heb 2:11; 3:14; 2 Pet 1:4). This is the mission that Jesus Christ fulfilled in the divine plan of redemption, which was made by the triune God before the foundation of the world.

The uniqueness of Christ's mediatorial office is emphasized in 1 Timothy 2:5—"one mediator." Having defined the meaning of the term "mediator" and having seen that meaning in relation to the work of Jesus Christ, we need to consider that He stands alone and unique in the place of mediatorship. "There is . . . one mediator between God and men" (v. 5)—the implied meaning is "one mediator only." There is only one God, and there is only one mediator between God and man. He alone uniquely effected mediation and reconciliation between God and mankind by His substitutionary death on Calvary's cross (see 2 Cor 5:18-21; 1 Pet 2:24; 3:18). Before bowing His head in death, Jesus said, "It is finished" (John 19:30). He had established reconciliation between the holy heavenly Father and His sinful creatures.

Christ alone did this and is, therefore, the only One who can effectively mediate between God and us. There is no other mediator. No other is needed, and none other can qualify. Christ, and Christ alone, filled this office.

Neither is any supplemental mediator needed or to be found. It is an arrogant violation of the revealed Gospel to assume mediatorship or to ascribe it to another. It is also a false assumption to stipulate the need for a supplemental mediator. Any human being professing to be such a go-between imposes on God's provision for salvation.

At the risk of being repetitious, I reiterate the fact that Christ alone qualified to atone for the sins of man, and He alone died to make restitution for man. By the one supreme sacrifice of Himself, He paid the penalty and made reconciliation between God and man possible.

There is no other way for people to reach God and to be reconciled to Him except through Jesus Christ. This is a profound, fundamental missionary truth. Just as there is only one God and people must come to know this God, there is only one mediator between God and man, and poeple can not know or approach God unless they do so through this divine mediator, Jesus Christ.

Unless sinful people know Jesus Christ as their sin-bearer and redeemer, the Bible states that they cannot truly come to God. It positively declares that there is "none other name under heaven given among men, whereby we **must be** saved" (Acts 4:12). It also says, "This is the record, that God hath given to us eternal life, and this life is in his Son. He that hath the Son hath life; and he that hath not the Son of God hath not life" (1 John 5:11,12). Jesus said concerning Himself, "I am the way, the truth, and the life: no man cometh unto the Father, but by me" (John 14:6). He also stated, "I am the door: by me if any man enter in, he shall be saved (10:9). Jesus was deeply aware that People could not come to God apart from Him, and this He clearly asserted.

This is why God desires all people to come to the knowledge of the truth. Apart from the knowledge of the truth of salvation in His Son, Jesus Christ, and apart from personal faith in Him, there can be no salvation. There is no other way to God. The God who loves and is concerned about all people and who has appointed and anointed His Son to be the mediator and Saviour for man, desires this knowledge to be brought within the reach of all people. Our Christian mission is to bring this knowledge to all the world.

As soon as any believer recognizes that Jesus Christ alone is the mediator between God and man and the only Redeemer of man, he must acknowledge the obligation of the mission to evangelize the world. Biblical theology inevitably involves missions. To acknowledge the uniqueness of Christ's role as man's Redeemer and at the same time deny or show indifference to the obligation of world evangelization is clearly inconsistent and contradictory.

Each of us must ask himself: Does my desire correspond with the desire of God? Does my confession of Jesus Christ as the one and only Saviour of man drive me to participate in the Christian world mission? Is it my desire that all people come to the knowledge of the truth of the Saviour in order that they may be saved? Do my actions correspond with my stated desire?

FIVE

The Universality of Christ's Atonement

So far we have considered the fact that believers are entreated to pray for all people. They are to pray especially for all who are in authority so that God's servants may be able to quietly and peacefully serve God and carry on His work in the world without deceit or dishonesty. We have considered the strong emphasis given to the truth that there is only one God. Then we noted that 1 Timothy 2:1-8 also makes it clear that God loves all people and desires that they be saved. The preceding chapter considered the unique office of Jesus Christ as the sole mediator between God and man.

In this chapter we will consider the fifth major truth set forth in this passage—the universality of Christ's atoning work. "[He] gave himself a ransom for all, to be testified in due time" (v. 6). The wonderful fact that He atoned for the sins of all is positively stated.

Sin demanded a ransom. In true Christian theology this fact is recognized as inevitable and inescapable. In the passage we are studying it is stated that Jesus "gave himself a ransom for all" (v. 6). This is simply because sin demanded a ransom.

The word "ransom" used in this passage and throughout the New Testament is a very significant one. The English word comes from the Latin root *redi-*

mere, from re and emere —"to take or buy"—therefore meaning "to buy back." *Webster's New Collegiate Dictionary* gives us this meaning of the verb *ransom:* "to free from captivity or punishment by paying a price." The noun form means "a consideration paid or demanded for the redemption of a captured person." "Ransom" is an accurate translation of the Greek word *lutron,* which the best lexicons define as "the price for redeeming (paid for slaves, for captives, for the ransom of a life)." The verb form is defined as "to release on receipt of ransom; to redeem, liberate by payment of ransom, to deliver."

But in this passage and in numerous other New Testament passages a compound form of the word is used. The preposition *anti,* the Greek word for "instead of" or "in place of," is attached as a prefix to *lutron.* It is the preposition of price, bargain or exchange, and this meaning is traceable in every New Testament passage where it occurs (see Matt 2:22; Luke 11:11; Heb 12:16). So when we are told that Jesus "gave himself a ransom" (1 Tim 2:6), the meaning is that He gave Himself as mankind's redemption price for sin. He died in our place. Dr. A. H. Strong, in his *Systematic Theology,* unequivocally says, *"Antilutron* equals substitutionary ransom."

Another common Greek preposition, *huper,* is usually translated "for" and means "in behalf of" or "for the benefit of." In this passage in Timothy, both these Greek prepositions are interwoven, emphasizing the marvelous fact that Christ gave Himself to be the ransom price for sinners and that He did this in behalf of, and for the benefit of, all mankind.

In Bible times ransoms were paid for three different purposes. They were paid to procure pardon for a legal offender, or a transgressor of the law. In a certain sense we still do this today. For example, when a man commits a misdemeanor, a relatively minor violation of the law, the court may impose a fine on him to make amends for his crime. Otherwise, he must go to jail. A judge's verdict is sometimes expressed as "One hundred dollars or thirty days in jail." If the person involved is unable to pay the fine, jail is inevitable unless someone else volunteers to pay the fine for him. The fine paid by his friend is then a kind of ransom. In ancient times a wealthy person would sometimes pay to deliver offenders in whom they took a personal interest.

A second type of ransom is the price paid for the release of a captive. In this generation it is fairly common for persons to be captured and held for some type of ransom, usually money. The captors may threaten to kill the captive unless the stipulated sum is paid for his or her release. The price fixed for the release is called "ransom money."

A third reason for which ransoms were paid in ancient times was to free slaves from bondage. Slavery has periodically been practiced in many parts of the world and was fairly common in the Roman Empire in New Testament times. Sometimes a wealthy person, for reasons known only to himself or out of compassion for a slave, would pay the slaveholder the price fixed on that slave and then graciously grant him his liberty. The spiritual application of this meaning of "ransom" to humanity is very fitting and magnifies the wonder and glory of our redemption in Jesus Christ.

Theologians have pointed our various scriptural methods of representing the atonement. Augustus H. Strong says, "We may classify the Scripture representations [of the atonement] according as they conform to moral, commercial, legal or sacrificial analogies" (Sys-

tematic Theology [Valley Forge: Judson, 1907], p. 716).
"Moral representation" refers to the atonement as a
provision originating in God's love and which man-
ifests this love to the universe; also as an example of
unselfish love, to secure our deliverance (see John 3:16;
Rom 5:8; 2 Cor 5:15; Eph 5:25-27; 1 John 4:9).

"Commercial representation" means that the
atonement is described as a ransom paid to free us from
the bondage of sin (see Matt 20:28; Mark 10:45; 1 Tim
2:6; 1 Cor 6:20).

The term "legal representation"describes the
atonement as an act of obedience to the law which
sinners had violated, a penalty borne in order to rescue
the guilty. It is also an exhibition of God's righteous-
ness, necessary to show the purpose of His work in the
pardon and restoration of sinners. In Matthew 3:15;
Luke 12:50; Romans 4:25; 5:19; 2 Corinthians 5:21; Galatians 4:4-5; Philippians 2:8 and many other passages,
Christ's death is represented as demanded by God's
law and by His divine order of government.

The term "sacrificial" describes the atonement as a
work of priestly mediation which reconciles God to
man, a sin offering presented on behalf of transgres-
sors, a propitiation which satisfies the demands of violated holiness and a substitution of Christ's obedience
and suffering for ours. Romans 5:10; 2 Corinthians
5:18, 19; Ephesians 2:16; Colossians 1:20; Hebrews
9:11, 12 and other passages show that Christ's death
was demanded by God's attribute of justice or holiness,
if sinners are to be saved. An examination of these
passages shows that, while the ways in which Christ's
atoning work is described are in part derived from
moral, commercial, and legal illustrations, the prevail-
ing language is that of sacrifice.

The theory that sacrifice is essentially the presentation of a gift to deity is foreign to the Scriptures. The true meaning of scriptural sacrifice is that of satisfaction of an offended God, or propitiation offered to violated holiness. The concept of the substitutionary suffering and death of the innocent for the deserved punishment of the guilty is clear in both the Old and New Testament scriptures. The Mosaic sacrifices were symbolic of the vicarious suffering and death of Christ, and they secured forgiveness and acceptance with God only as they were offered in true penitence and with faith in God's ordained method of salvation.

Throughout the Bible the concept of sacrifices is that of satisfaction by substitution. The sacrifices expressed the consciousness that sin involves guilt; guilt exposes man to the righteous wrath of God; without atonement for guilt there is no forgiveness; and through the suffering of another the transgressions of the sinner may be paid for. A simple deduction from scriptural facts is that the death of Christ is a vicarious offering provided by God's love to satisfy an internal demand of His divine holiness and to remove an obstacle in His divine mind to the renewal and pardon of sinners.

People have offended God. They have broken His law and made themselves offenders. They have been captivated by sin and have been made its bondslaves. Jesus Christ paid the ransom to relieve and release them. "[He] gave himself a ransom for all" (1 Tim 2:6). He did it voluntarily. He came into the world for the purpose of giving Himself a ransom for the sins of man. The purpose of His coming is recorded in Mark 10:45: "The Son of man came not to be ministered unto, but to minister, and to give his life a ransom for many." And at tremendous cost He vicariously paid the ransom for human sin. In the Garden of Gethsemane, in the anguish of His soul, His sweat became like drops of blood as He prepared to take the cup that represented the combined guilt and penalty of the world's sin. Shortly after that came His anguished cry from Golgotha's cross, "My God, my God, why hast thou forsaken me?" (Matt 27:46). Yet He gave Himself to do this for us.

"[He] gave himself a ransom for all" (1 Tim 2:6). His substitutionary death on the cross was not just for "His own" people—not for any particular nation or part of the world and not for the people of any one race. He gave Himself a ransom for all to save and deliver people everywhere from their sins by His own divine grace and all-sufficient power.

Was Christ's atoning death truly universal and unlimited? Or was it limited to the elect only? This is a question over which theologians have long battled. In the past as well as in the present, some have been very emphatic in affirming that the atonement is strictly limited to those who have been predestined to salvation. Though John Calvin is often cited as the proponent of this view of the atonement, I regard this assertion to be incorrect. Calvin himself declared that Christ suffered for the sins of the whole world. How can anyone justly think otherwise in the light of Scripture passages such as 1 John 2:2? This verse says, "He is the propitiation for our [believers'] sins; and not for our's only, but also for the sins of the whole world." No one has ever challenged the translation of this passage; in fact, all familiar translations render it essentially the same as the King James Version.

Dr. J. W. Northrup, of a previous generation, presented the atoning work of Christ as universal in three aspects: (1) It reconciled God to the whole race, apart from personal transgression. (2) It secured the bestowment on all of common grace and the means of common grace. (3) It guaranteed the bestowment of eternal life on all who would use common grace.

Mere religion, of whatever kind, can never save man. No humanly obtained status can make man acceptable to God, because we are guilty and depraved sinners. But Jesus provided the ransom for all. As our text passage states, "[He] gave himself a ransom for all" (1 Tim 2:6). This means that He provided a ransom for all mankind, for all the sons of Adam, for the entire human race. The prophet Isaiah wrote: "All we like sheep have gone astray; we have turned every one to his own way; and the Lord hath laid on him the iniquity of us all" (Isa 53:6). He gave Himself as a ransom for us on Calvary's cross, and it is His purpose, the longing and desire of His heart, that He might deliver mankind from the penalty of their offenses against His holy Father's government. His desire is to set people free from the bonds of iniquity in which they have been ensnared and captivated. He longs to release people from the slavery of sin. He gave Himself a ransom for all of mankind.

I emphasize again that He did this for only one reason—pure, unselfish, divine love. We implied earlier that love is basically God's self-communication. It cost Jesus a tremendous price to make atonement for the sins of the world. What a tragedy that multitudes of the people for whom He died, the multitudes of men, women, and children for whom He made full and sufficient atonement, still do not know. They live on in the awful slavery and under the terrible guilt of sin. They go on in their satanic captivity, sighing, crying, and longing for deliverance. They do not know Christ already paid the ransom for them all and by simple faith in Him they could be set free. Our Christian responsibility is to tell them. If Christ loved the world enough to give Himself as a ransom for all, surely we who are His people ought to have enough of that same divine love in our hearts to do everything in our power to tell others the story.

SIX

Universal Proclamation of the Gospel

The statement we are about to consider immediately follows the declaration that Christ gave Himself a ransom for all and made atonement for the sins of all mankind. This highly significant statement is "to be testified in due time" (1 Tim 2:6).

Four important questions concerning this statement must be answered: What is the meaning and implication of the word *testify*? What is to be testified to? To whom is the testimony to be given? When is the "due time" for the testimony?

Our English word *testify* means "to make a statement based on personal knowledge or belief; to bear witness; to make known; to give evidence of; to declare under oath." It is a very exact equivalent of the Greek word used in this text—*márturion*—which means "to be a witness to bear witness, to affirm that one has seen or heard or experienced something, or that he knows it because taught by divine revelation" (Thayer). "Testify" and "witness" are the same in the Greek language.

There are many references in the New Testament to the fact that Christians are the designated witnesses of Jesus Christ and the Gospel. In outlining the great plan of God, Jesus opened the understanding of the apostles to the Scriptures and showed them "that repentance and remission of sins **should be** preached in his name among all nations, **beginning** at Jerusalem" (Luke 24:47). He pointed out that they were witnesses. Just before His ascension into heaven, He again said to the apostles, "Ye shall be witnesses unto me . . . unto the uttermost part of the earth" (Acts 1:8). During His discourse to the disciples on the way to the Garden of Gethsemane He said, "Ye also shall bear witness, because ye have been with me from the beginning" (John 15:27).

The great apostle Paul considered himself to be Christ's witness to the world—to his own Jewish people and preeminently to the Gentiles. When he stood before King Agrippa to defend himself against his accusers, he gave personal testimony about how he had become a Christian. He said, "Having therefore obtained help of God, I continue unto this day, witnessing both to small and great, saying none other things than those which the prophets and Moses did say should come: that Christ should suffer, and that he should be the first that should rise from the dead, and should shew light unto the people, and to the Gentiles" (Acts 26:22-23).

Our text passage clearly affirms that, following Christ's giving Himself as a ransom for the sins of all and making an atonement for mankind, the witness of this must be borne to all people.

Though speakers and writers have pointed out that our English word "martyr" comes from the Greek word "*martus*," this fact does not imply that being a witness necessarily implies martyrdom. However, the origin of our word "martyr" probably stems from the fact that many Gospel witnesses throughout church history were martyred because of their testimony for Christ. And it is true that those who take the gospel to the peoples of our world **must be willing to lay** down their lives for their faith.

In the book of the Revelation, mention is made of "the blood of the saints [God's people], and . . . **the** blood of the martyrs of Jesus [witnesses for Jesus]" (17:6). In chapter 20 John wrote: "I saw the souls **of** them that were beheaded for the witness of Jesus" (v.4). Because Jesus' witnesses have often been killed, some of the early English translators coined the word *martyr* from the Greek word for "witness." In our own generation some of His witnesses have been martyred for their testimony; more may yet have to follow.

What is the testimony that is to be borne? What is to be testified to or made known? The answer has already been implied. The redemptive work of Jesus Christ for mankind, the Gospel of salvation, is to be made known. This conclusion is obvious from 1 Timothy 2:6: "Who [Christ] gave himself a ransom for all, to be testified in due time." The "what" of the testimony is not at all ambiguous; it obviously relates to the redemptive work of Christ our Saviour; He, the eternal Son of God, gave Himself a ransom for all and became the Saviour of the world. This must be made known to the world. So the testimony referred to as a divine requirement is evangelization—the proclamation of the Gospel of Jesus Christ to the creatures for whom He died.

After many years of missionary endeavor, the apostle Paul stated that the ministry which he had received from the Lord Jesus was "to testify the gospel of the grace of God" (Acts 20:24). When Jesus opened the understanding of His disciples to the Scriptures following His resurrection, He said, "It is written, and thus it behoved Christ to suffer, and to rise from the dead the third day: and that repentance and remission of sins should be preached in his name among all nations, beginning at Jerusalem. And ye are witnesses of these things" (Luke 24:46-48). Jesus Himself made it clear that the witness, or testimony, to be borne by His disciples concerned repentance and remission of sins for mankind in His name.

Jesus pointed out two fundamental truths of Scripture, basic to the understanding of the Scriptures—the necessity of His atoning death and the necessity for the evangelization of the world by the Church. The same two truths are emphasized in 2 Corinthians 5:18, 19: "And all things are of God, who hath reconciled us to himself by Jesus Christ, and hath given to us the ministry of reconciliation; to wit [namely], that God was in Christ, reconciling the world unto himself, not imputing their trespasses unto them; and hath committed unto us the word of reconciliation." This passage emphasizes the fact that God was, in Christ, reconciling the world to Himself and that He has committed to us the responsibility of proclaiming reconciliation to all people.

Two very significant words are used in 2 Corinthians 5 to describe the ministry of reconciliation. One of them is found in verse 11: "Knowing therefore the terror [reverential fear] of the Lord, we persuade men." The word "persuade" means ""to move by argument, entreaty, or expostulation to a belief, position, or course of action." Wherever Paul and his missionary companions went throughout the world, they were engaged in persuading people that Jesus Christ was the Son of God and the Saviour of mankind.

The other significant word in this passage, "beseech," occurs in verse 20. This means "to beg for urgently or anxiously; to request earnestly, implore." The divinely commissioned task of the Church of Jesus

Christ is to do everything possible by every legitimate means to persuade people of all nations to turn to the Saviour. Believers are to beseech non-believers to be reconciled to God through Him.

In this Corinthian passage, the apostle affirmed that we are Christ's ambassadors. An ambassador is the highest-level appointed official of state sent to another land to effect a reconciliation between the two states involved. He is to use every possible argument and persuasion. This is our high and holy Christian office, and we must not do less than an earthly ambassador. Paul added this further testimony: "We pray you in Christ's stead, be ye reconciled to God" (v. 20). This is yet another way of expressing the idea of desiring, longing for, asking, or begging.

First Timothy 2:6 says, "To be testified in due time." What does "due time" mean? What time is meant? What specific period of time is this "due time"?

The literal reading in the Greek would be "the testimony in its own times." The obvious meaning is that the testimony of the ransom is to be given in its own time. In other words, the gift of Christ as a ransom is the substance of the testimony, which must be made in its proper season. This is the precise explanation given by Marvin R. Vincent in his *Word Studies in the New Testament.* The same Greek terminology is used again in 1 Timothy 6:15: "Which in his times he shall shew, who is the blessed and only Potentate, the King of kings, and Lord of Lords." The term is also found in Titus 1:3 and in Galatians 6:9.

Clearly, the thought is that since salvation has been provided for all people, since Christ has made atonement for the sins of the world, and since redemption is finished, now is the proper time to give this testimony to the world. Christ has provided a ransom for the sins of the world, and people need to hear the message of the atonement and to be given the invitation to salvation and reconciliation to God through His appointed Saviour.

In the epistle to the Galatians the apostle Paul stated, "When the fulness of the time was come, God sent forth his Son, made of a woman, made under the law, to redeem them that were under the law" (4:4). Several recent English translations render this phrase "when the proper time," "at the proper time," or "in the proper time."

In his epistle to the Ephesians, Paul projected a mystery which had been revealed to him by God but had previously been hidden from mankind. This mystery, revealed in this present time, is that the Gentiles would become members and heirs in the Body of Christ and full partakers of God's promises in the Gospel. As a minister to the Gentiles, Paul's task was to make all people see "what is the fellowship of the mystery, which from the beginning of the world hath been hid in God" (Eph 3:9).

The divine plan of salvation is being worked out by God in dispensations, or different periods of time. He called Abraham to become the father of a separate nation, which was to be His channel for worldwide blessing. Those blessings included preserving the knowledge of Himself as the one true God among mankind, giving His written Scriptures to the world, and ultimately bringing the Saviour into the world (see Gen 12:3; 22:18; Gal 3:16).

Many specific laws, such as the dietary laws, were given to the nation of Israel so they would remain a separate people and be preserved as God's divinely chosen channel. All the Old Testament ordinances and sacrifices were a preparation for the coming of Jesus Christ and this sacrifice for the sins of the world. The Mosaic system showed that people were sinners and needed reconciliation. It demonstrated that reconciliation could be accomplished only through the shedding of blood. The Old Testament priesthood was a type of the universal priesthood of the Lord Jesus Christ as the one mediator between God and man.

There was a proper time in the plan of God for Christ to come into this world and give Himself a ransom for mankind's sin. And there is a proper time in the plan of God for the proclamation of salvation in His name to all the nations of the world. That due time is now. It began on the day of Pentecost when the disciples, empowered by the Holy Spirit, began to proclaim the message to all who were gathered in Jerusalem. It has continued throughout the Dispensation of Grace. When Jesus gave His commission to the apostles, His command to preach repentance and remission of sins in His name among all nations was based on the Scriptures. He instructed His disciples, "But tarry ye in the city of Jerusalem, until ye be endued with power from on high" (Luke 24:49).

Prior to His ascension into heaven, He said to the apostles, "Ye shall receive power, after that [when] the Holy Ghost is come upon you: and ye shall be witnesses unto me both in Jerusalem, and in all Judaea, and in Samaria, and unto the uttermost part of the earth" (Acts 1:8). Obviously, He was referring to the day of Pentecost. On the day of Pentecost the Holy Spirit came to earth to take up His abode in the Body of Christ—the church—and empowered that Body to carry out the evangelization of the world.

The day of Pentecost marked the beginning of the "due time" for the proclamation of Christ's gospel of redeeming grace to a lost world. This is the dispensation in God's divine plan for the world to be evangelized. This is the Church age. This is the age of the Holy Spirit, who came to the Church at Pentecost to enable it to bear the witness of the gospel to the uttermost part of the earth. This is the age in which Jesus has commanded, and is expecting, His Church to go into all the world and preach the Gospel to every creature.

This "due time" in the divine plan began on the day of Pentecost. In this day it is well past due time for multitudes. The hour is late. The shadows over our dispensational day are lengthening. The night is approaching when we will no longer be able to work. The watchword for us is "Now is the accepted time" (2 Cor 6:2).

Some have erroneously projected the time for world evangelization into a future age—after the Church is removed from the earth and the Tribulation begins or during the millennial Kingdom. But who, in the light of Luke 24:45-49 and Acts 1:4-8, can honestly place such an interpretation on God's revealed plan? The time for the witness of the gospel and the evangelization of the world was to begin on the day of Pentecost and is to be continued by the Church during this age.

To whom is the witness to be given? The answer to this has already been quite clearly implied. Obviously, the witness is to be given to those for whom the ransom was paid. And since the Word tells us specifically that He "gave himself a ransom for all, to be testified in due time" (1 Tim 2:6), the witness must be given to all humanity, all races, all nations, all peoples, all the earth. He died for all, and He desires that all be told. This fact is emphasized throughout the Scriptures.

But multitudes still live and die in many places of the earth without ever being told of the redeeming work of Jesus Christ. For multitudes of people in the world it is as if Jesus had never made atonement for their sins or brought the grace of God within their reach simply because they have never heard the message. In its failure to tell the gospel of Jesus Christ to the whole world the Church has sadly failed humanity and tragically failed God.

The witness of Jesus Christ to all the peoples of the world is an integral and vital part of the divine plan of salvation. It is not something optional or volitional. It is not supplementary or auxiliary to the Gospel. The testimony of His Gospel to the whole world is as essential to the plan of redemption as the ransom act He Himself made on the cross. He died for all. We recognize at once how necessary this is. But we have not so readily recognized that He is "to be testified in due time" (v. 6) to all, although this is equally important and equally essential to human salvation. Just as people could not have been saved apart from the atoning death of Christ, neither can they be saved apart from the knowledge of what he has done for them. They must hear and believe in order to be saved. Passages such as Mark 16:16; Luke 24:47; John 1:12; 10:1; 14:6; 20:31; Acts 4:12; 16:31; Romans 10:12-15; and 1 John 5:12 make this clear.

The universal salvation proclaimed in our time by neoorthodox theologians—that since Christ died to make atonement for all people, all are consequently saved—is not scriptural. This view of redemption describes the Christian mission as merely informing people that they have been reconciled to God by Jesus Christ and are, therefore, His Children. Contrary to this, the Scriptures make it clear that the Gospel must be preached to **people and that individuals** must exercise specific faith in the Lord Jesus Christ by their own will in order to be reconciled to God. This is precisely why the apostle Paul stated that God was, in Christ, reconciling the world to Himself and has committed to us the ministry of reconciliation. Therefore, we must plead with people to be reconciled to God (see 2 Cor 5:18-21).

Jesus has removed the barrier of sin and guilt between God and man by His substitutionary death. But the barrier still standing between multitudes of people and God is lack of knowledge about that glorious provision. Multitudes of people are separated from God in the darkness of sin because they do not know the blessed work done for them by the man Jesus Christ.

It is clear throughout the Scriptures that God does not violate the dignity of human will, and this applies to our decision concerning salvation. Christ died to make salvation possible for all, and as people, through the knowledge of the Gospel and by their own will, trust Him as their Redeemer, they are reconciled to God and born into His spiritual kingdom. The great truth of the universal proclamation of the gospel so strongly emphasized in 1 Timothy 2:1-8 is also seen in many other parts of Scripture as well.

In 1 Timothy 2:1-8 we are told that God desires all people to be saved by coming to the knowledge of the truth. Jesus Christ became a man in order to be our Redeemer, and in His death He gave Himself a ransom for the sins of all. He is the only mediator between God and man. Therefore, He is the only way by which people can be reconciled to God. The apostle emphasized that Christ's atoning work must be testified to mankind. The due time for this is now. It began on the day of Pentecost, when the Holy Spirit came to the

Church to empower His people to be witnesses of Christ to the uttermost part of the earth. For many parts of the world, the time is now past due!

SEVEN

Human Instrumentality

In this chapter we will consider the final basic truth in this Scripture passage—the clear fact that human instrumentality is God's method of operation in the work of evangelism. After stating the fact that Jesus Christ, as the Redeemer for all people, is to be testified to the world in due time, the apostle added, "Whereunto I am ordained a preacher and an apostle, (I speak the truth in Christ, and lie not;) a teacher of the Gentiles" (1 Tim 2:7).

"Whereunto I am ordained," or "for this purpose I was appointed," of course, refers to the immediately preceding statement—"to be testified in due time" (v.6). Paul involved himself as a part of the witnessing agency. In so doing he also involved other believers. The testimony of the gospel to the world is to be given by those who have been redeemed. This is God's plan; He has no other.

God's plan for using human instruments to do His work in the world is declared and emphasized throughout the Bible. We need only to recall such statements as the one in 2 Corinthians 5: "And all things are of God, who hath reconciled us to himself by Jesus Christ, and hath given to us the ministry of reconciliation; to wit, that God was in Christ, reconciling the world unto himself, not imputing their trespasses unto them; and hath committed unto us the word of reconciliation. Now then we are ambassadors for

Christ, as though God did beseech you by us" (vv. 18-20).

Christ was ordained to be the agent in redemption, but His people are the instruments for proclaiming it. He made provision for the reconciliation of sinful humanity, but we are His chosen ambassadors to publish the Good News.

Luke 24:45-48, a very familiar and important passage, also points out this truth: "Then opened he their understanding, that they might understand the scriptures, and said unto them, Thus it is written, and thus it behoved Christ to suffer, and to rise from the dead the third day: and that repentance and remission of sins should be preached in his name among all nations, beginning at Jerusalem. And ye are witnesses of these things." He showed His disciples from the Scriptures that it was necessary for Him "to suffer, and to rise from the dead" (v. 46)—that is atonement. He also stated "that repentance and remission of sins should be preached in his name among all nations" (v. 47)—that's evangelization. He immediately added, "Ye are witnesses of these things" (v. 48)—that's human instrumentality.

In speaking to His disciples after His resurrection, Jesus said, "As my Father hath sent me, even so send I you (John 20:21). This is God's decreed method and plan of salvation: His Son was sent to be the world's sin-bearer, and His servants are sent to tell the world the story. He has no other agency, no other means for world evangelization, except human instruments—men, women, and children who have themselves been redeemed through faith in the Lord Jesus Christ.

We pointed out earlier that Christ alone could qualify to pay the ransom for sin and become the mediator between God and man. No one else was able to do this. It was necessary that He fulfill that part of redemption's demands. But proclaiming the Good News to mankind is something that human beings can do. The only requirement is that they must be redeemed human beings, willing to do God's will as His servants.

The Bible refers to two bodies in connection with Jesus Christ; both are divine instruments for human redemption. Both are miraculous, and both are mysterious.

First, He was given a physical body, miraculously formed in the womb of a virgin, so that He could suffer physically for the sins of man and make atonement for them. In heaven, before He came into the world to fulfill His part of redemption's plan, Jesus said to the Father, "Sacrifice and offering [animal sacrifices of the Mosaic ritual] thou wouldest not [you have not desired], but a body hast thou prepared me: in burnt-offerings and sacrifices for sin thou hast had no pleasure. Then said I, Lo, I come . . . to do thy will, O God" (Heb 10:5-7). He knew that, in the body prepared for Him in Mary's womb, He would undergo terrible sacrifice and suffering for the sins of the world. Yet He said, "I come . . . to do thy will, O God" (v. 7).

Second, the Scriptures show that He has yet another Body—a spiritual one: "The church, which is his body" (Eph 1:22-23; see Col 1:18). In this spiritual body the second great part of redemption's work is to be completed—the evangelization of the world, or the proclamation of redemption to all nations.

The part that Christ alone could do, He did. He finished His part. The part which redeemed people can do has been assigned to them, but it is yet unfinished.

Note Paul's personal testimony in declaring that he was ordained a preacher and an apostle, a proclaimer of Jesus' redemptive work. The word "preacher" literally means "a heralder," or "a proclaimer." Jesus' command was "Go ye into all the world, and preach [proclaim, herald] the gospel to every creature" (Mark 16:15). Preachers are, of course, human beings; they are the witnesses of Christ's saving grace to the world around them to the uttermost part of the earth.

But this command is not limited to a select group of clergymen or to professional missionaries. All Christians are to be heralds of the message of Jesus Christ to all the people around them. Some, like Paul, are ordained of God to leave their home and go to other areas to make Jesus Christ known, but all believers are to be His witnesses.

Paul stated that not only was he ordained a preacher, he was also an apostle. Paul knew that he was an apostle (see Acts 22:21; 1 Tim 1:1). A missionary is, in a sense, an apostle. The word "missionary" is the exact Latin equivalent for the Greek word "apostle." Both words have the same meaning—"one who has been sent." Jesus said to His disciples after His resurrection, "As my Father hath sent me, even so send I you" (John 20:21).

The apostle Paul had been ordained of God as a special gospel witness to the Gentile nations. He testified that he was sent to the Gentiles "to open their eyes, and to turn them from darkness to light, and from the power of Satan unto God" (Acts 26:18). From the time of his conversion, God had made it clear that Paul was a chosen vessel to bear His name before kings, Gentiles, and the people of Israel (9:15). Throughout the history of the Church and up to the present time, God has been calling people to be His special witnesses in heathen lands and nations.

The third word the apostle used to describe himself is "teacher." This refers to an instructor, an informer, one who discloses or dispenses knowledge. This is our task as Christians. We are to go into the world as instruments in God's great plan of salvation to dispense, disclose, and make known the knowledge of Jesus Christ and the way of salvation through faith in Him. God is still calling men and women to be teachers to the Gentiles in pagan lands.

The divine plan embraces human instrumentality, but there is also an affirmative personal call to specific service for the individual being used. Paul's testimony of having been ordained, or set apart, for the specific ministry of carrying the Gospel to the heathen and teaching them the true faith clearly indicates his consciousness. of a personal call from God. And this immediately points to Acts 13, where the specific call of the Holy Spirit came to the Church and to Paul and Barnabas. They were to launch out on their first foreign gifts, training, and personality; I, all that I am and all that I have; I have been ordained of God to go to the called them . . . So they, being sent forth by the Holy Ghost, departed" (vv. 2, 4).

Note the apostle's words in our text passage: "Whereunto I am ordained" (1 Tim 2:7). In effect, Paul was saying, "I, Paul, an individual Christian person: I, one who has been saved by God's grace; I, a child of God through redemption; I, with my peculiar talents, gifts, training and personality; I, all that I am and all that I have; I have been ordained of God to go to the heathen." This was a personal calling. God has ordained in a general and overall manner the plan that Christians should be His instruments in world evangelization, but He calls individuals to specific responsibilities and places in order to fulfill His divine program.

And who does God call? He calls many. Indeed, He may call any. He may be calling you to a special place in this great ministry of proclaiming the ransom Jesus Christ made for a lost world. If you think you are hearing His call, will you like Samuel say, "Speak, Lord; for thy servant heareth"? (1 Sam 3:9). Until Samuel responded, he was confused and uncertain, not sure of the call of God. But once he responded, saying, "Speak, Lord; for thy servant heareth" (v.9), God made the call clear and distinct. This is God's manner of calling people.

> Let none hear you idly saying,
>   "There is nothing I can do,"
> While the souls of men are dying,
>   And the Master calls for you.
> Take the task He gives you gladly,
>   Let His work your pleasure be;
> Answer quickly when He calleth,
>   "Here am I send me, send me!"
>
> —DANIEL MARCH